THE SAGAJO EXPERIENCE
RECIPES FOR LIFESTYLE & ENTERTAINING

COPYRIGHT

INTRODUCTION

I grew up in the beautiful Caribbean twin-island nation known as Trinidad and Tobago, a place of diverse cultures that has given us a rich smorgasbord of foods, spices, seasonings, flavors, and an abundance of fruits and vegetables. My story is simple: it starts with my mother Alma, a successful chef who entered many international culinary competitions and won many times. My mother's achievements really inspired me to become a top-notch chef: no doubt she was my biggest influence. Under her tutelage cooking, baking and preparing food of all kinds was the norm, as my family entertained and celebrated every birthday, anniversary, special traditional holiday and more. Having a lavish table of food, desserts, flowers and all the trimmings was not unusual, for we cooked to celebrate life itself.

As the first born, I was tasked with helping my mother with the chores and preparing meals for our family, and when my mother had to cater for her many clients I sometimes would help. I think that is where I developed my passion and love for cooking. Whilst most young girls were having fun with their peers I was having fun creating my own dishes, baking cakes, frosting, piping borders and making roses for decorating cakes. As a little girl, I had no clue that I was preparing for my future calling. At the age of sixteen, I had my first big order of creating a birthday cake. What I created and put together was beautiful and everyone enjoyed it. Soon I was doing occasion cakes for friends, and anyone who would be brave enough to have a sixteen year old create a cake for them. The great feeling of accomplishment encouraged me to go further, and I thoroughly enjoyed producing the beautiful ideas that kept popping up in my mind. I was loving every moment in the kitchen.

As life would have it, I met and dated a wonderful young man named Gordon. A wonderful and very brave man indeed, because I somehow convinced him to become the taste tester for my experiments with gastronomy. I cooked and plated my dishes, and he ate every one with excitement. Let's just say he was good for my ego - nothing ever tasted bad for him, he loved and enjoyed every meal. Yes indeed, he lifted me high. I'm sure there were few items that were not so tasty, but with him, I would never know.

Our love for food was food enough for the love that grew between us. Eventually, we both found ourselves migrating from Trinidad and Tobago to Canada to start our family. One of the challenges we faced was the cold weather, but thankfully what we felt for each other got us through very chilly days. As we got married and started our lives together, I created and cooked more interesting dishes, working with the budget I had at the time. Being innovative meant that I could make grocery shopping great fun, and even more of an adventure as I discovered the vegetables, fruits and other ingredients that were rarely available in the islands.

After a few years our daughter Sasha was born and we were overjoyed. Even as a new mom, I would try my best to plan and prepare enjoyable dining experiences, making every mealtime special for my loved ones. It would mean taking my new-born to the grocery with me, a real challenge with the fierce winter weather. Nonetheless, I always managed my time. After our daughter was fed, while she slept, I would prepare a delicious meal for the family that we would all gather around. Cooking was actually a great de-stresser for me. This might be hard to believe, but it's true.

Over time our family grew. We had another daughter, Gabrielle, and our son, Jonathan. Needless to say life got busier than I could've imagined. I was a wife managing motherhood, cooking and managing our home. In our home, I was now the CEO - organiser, manager and head of human resources. During this time, Gordon was appointed to be the VP of the U.S.A. Operations for his company, which required us to relocate to New York. There were so many mixed emotions, but we eventually realised that another part of our lives was unfolding. We all got adjusted and settled in our new house in Long Island. As the new location CEO, I immersed myself into making it into our home and my office for private catering jobs.

The children were getting older, but I continued to make mealtimes special, setting the table for our family dinners and calling everyone to eat at the same time. This was a wonderful family bonding time as the children would say the sweetest things - "This tastes yummy mummy", "Delicious!" and "I'm going to eat all my veggies mom". This made me so happy, knowing that I created a wonderful meal for my family. I loved watching them eat and the smiles on their little faces brought joy to my heart.

This endorsement from my children fuelled my entrepreneurial spirit, and I decided to enroll in the Culinary School of Long Island, where I aimed to perfect my skills in the culinary arts of different regions. Certifying myself at this institution gave me such a great feeling of accomplishment. My family celebrated with me, and my dear Gordon was extremely happy that I achieved one of my desires. I expanded my catering to families and other people who knew me. Honing my skills even further with these occasions led to some good opportunities.

Life continued to bless us richly. Gordon was promoted again, which involved moving to Florida. Needless to say, the changes here caused some emotional upheaval as my much older children were sorry to lose the people they befriended, but we rallied through and began our lives anew in Boca Raton, Florida. Even as I am typing these memoirs, the tears start flowing down my cheek. I cannot believe how much and how rapidly life has changed. I appreciate all of the adventures and situations that we've gone through together.

I was employed as a teacher at West Boca High School, where I taught an adult education cooking and baking program. I enjoyed teaching so much, and experienced a different kind of joy in sharing my talent for cooking and baking with others. The experience inspired me to begin writing about the culinary arts. Then I decided to take on a job as the Assistant Pastry Chef in one of Florida's country clubs, which I enjoy immensely. However, as my husband spent time travelling with work, it became almost impossible for me to have family time because my job kept me very busy. I missed cooking and sitting around the table with my family, so I continued more private catering and private cooking lessons for a few clients. This enabled me to be at home and still engage in doing what I enjoy.

My book of recipes for lifestyle and entertaining has allowed me to share my recommendations for bringing family and friends together through the dining experience. My recipes are my personal creations, blending the Caribbean culinary know-how and the creative techniques I have learned from catering and teaching in the United States. They have been honed through much experimentation and re-engineering, and, above all else, they have been inspired by my love for gathering beloved family members and friends to my table. I hope that once you have this book, it brings you as much pleasure and happiness as it has brought me through the process of writing and producing it.

DEBBIE BERMENT CHEF SAGAJO

Debbie is professionally known as Chef Sagajo. The name "Sagajo" is one that was created from the first two letters of her children's names: Sasha, Gabrielle and Jonathan. It is for this reason that the name has a special meaning and place in her heart. Her children have been the prime inspiration for her brand as a chef and culinary expert.

Debbie's culinary career started early, for she was tasked with helping her mother prepare meals and, at times, assisting with the family's catering business. What started out as just helping mom, Debbie's relationship with the kitchen quickly blossomed into a passion, and at the age of sixteen, began creating her own flavors and decorating styles while baking cakes for her friends and family members. Her mother's inspiration and example gave her the foresight to explore her first love, and complete a professional certification as a trained Chef at a top Culinary School in the United States.

The way Chef Sagajo creates unique culinary experiences is with the selection of the finest ingredients, so she works with items and products she truly loves. These are prepared and blended perfectly into her recipes, to create dishes that awaken the palette to the deep, complex flavours and nutritious concoctions presented as works of art.

Chef Sagajo spends a great deal of time cooking, baking, testing and tasting in her kitchen. To her food is not simply making something that tastes good. The truth is, effective gastronomical science is important to our wellness and health. Preparing each ingredient to maximise its nutrient properties is important, and this is why Chef Sagajo takes special care in how she manoeuvres every aspect of the meal, ensuring no loss of food value in creating every single perfectly cooked and artfully presented dish.

She is grateful for her family, who has been her support system and a big part of why she is so happy. Cooking meals, entertaining friends and family while creating memories is what you can find Chef Sagajo doing everyday.

Chef Sagajo's personal credo is, "Do what you love and you never work a day in your life!"

'Do what
you love!'

DEDICATION

Dedication to my mother, Alma Wilson

Mom, for helping to guide my career in gastronomy, and for exemplifying dedication and a passion for all things food, I am grateful. You are the one who inspired me to cook using a distinctive medley of ingredients and techniques. Thank you for instilling in me an appreciation for the world of local spices and seasonings that set our dishes apart. Watching you in the kitchen motivated me to aim for the best in all that I did to bring people together through food and entertainment. Your legacy is in every recipe I create to show that

"Life is meant to taste and celebrate."

Thank you, Mom.

'Life is meant
to taste and
celebrate.'

TABLE OF CONTENTS

reakfast in Bed

husband travels often for work, so when we get the chance have a romantic meal together, I make the most of it! hether it's my master bedroom for breakfast in bed, or a sy spot in the living room or even the patio, I love to create an imate space for us to enjoy. A variety of candles, a few fresh ens & cushions, and aromatic flowers are a must to achieve s snugly feel.

hen it comes to a romantic breakfast in bed with my hubby, I ay true to the Sagajo essentials: fresh linen, warm throws, mfy cushions, flowers and of course, incredible food.

ll starts with setting the mood. I choose clean, minimal colors r the linen and throws on our bed. Think whites, creams, beiges d greys. Textured and patterned cushions help bring warmth d dimension to the set-up. Using fresh flowers is a great way add color without permanently altering the decor. Flowers hance the romantic mood with their delectable fragrance, so e meal is even more delicious and memorable. The sheer riety that is available means you can select a range of colors d or shapes to enhance any setting: Red Roses for anniversa- s, Pink Peonies for Valentine's Day, bright yellow Sunflowers ring in Spring or maybe a bouquet of your loved one's vorite.

This is where you can choose to be as colorful, creative and personal as you'd like. Adorn the room with some candles and you're ready to serve up the most romantic breakfast in bed!

Now let's talk about food. They say breakfast is the most important meal of the day but I think it's the most fabulous excuse to share champagne and carbs in the morning, without the guilt.

To my beautiful bed set-up, I lay out a tray of my husband's favorites- fluffy blueberry pancakes with warm maple & sage syrup, a bowl of sweet seasonal fruits and two cappuccinos, please! When we finally get around to finishing this wonderful meal, it's time to pop the bubbly and chat about the week ahead... Breakfast in bed is the perfect accompaniment to a morning spent reminiscing about family memories and to discuss our plans for times with grandkids. As well, if I'm lucky, I can convince my love that we absolutely need new dishware.

Fluffy Blueberry Pancakes

Preparation time: 10 minutes
Cooking time: 20 minutes
Yields 8-10 pancakes

2 ½ cups flour, leveled
3 tablespoons granulated sugar
1 teaspoon baking powder
1 teaspoon baking soda
2 teaspoons salt
2 ½ cups buttermilk
1 stick of butter melted, then cooled
2 egg yolks at room temperature
2 egg whites
Blueberries

- In a mixing bowl, combine flour, sugar, baking powder, baking soda, and salt.

- In a separate bowl, combine buttermilk, butter, egg yolks. Whisk together.

- Add the wet ingredients to the dry ingredients just to combine.

- Add the egg whites to the mixture and fold until fully incorporated.

- Rest the batter for 15-30 minutes. Do not skip this step! This will ensure the pancakes are light and fluffy.

- In a cast iron skillet, over medium heat, add a tablespoon of butter and melt.

- Using a ladle or measuring cup, spoon batter into the skillet.

- When bubbles appear, add blueberries. Flip and cook the other side. Approximately 2-3 minutes per side, until browned. Serve warm with a pat of butter and maple syrup.

Note: You can add any type of berry or even chocolate chips to the recipe to make it your own!

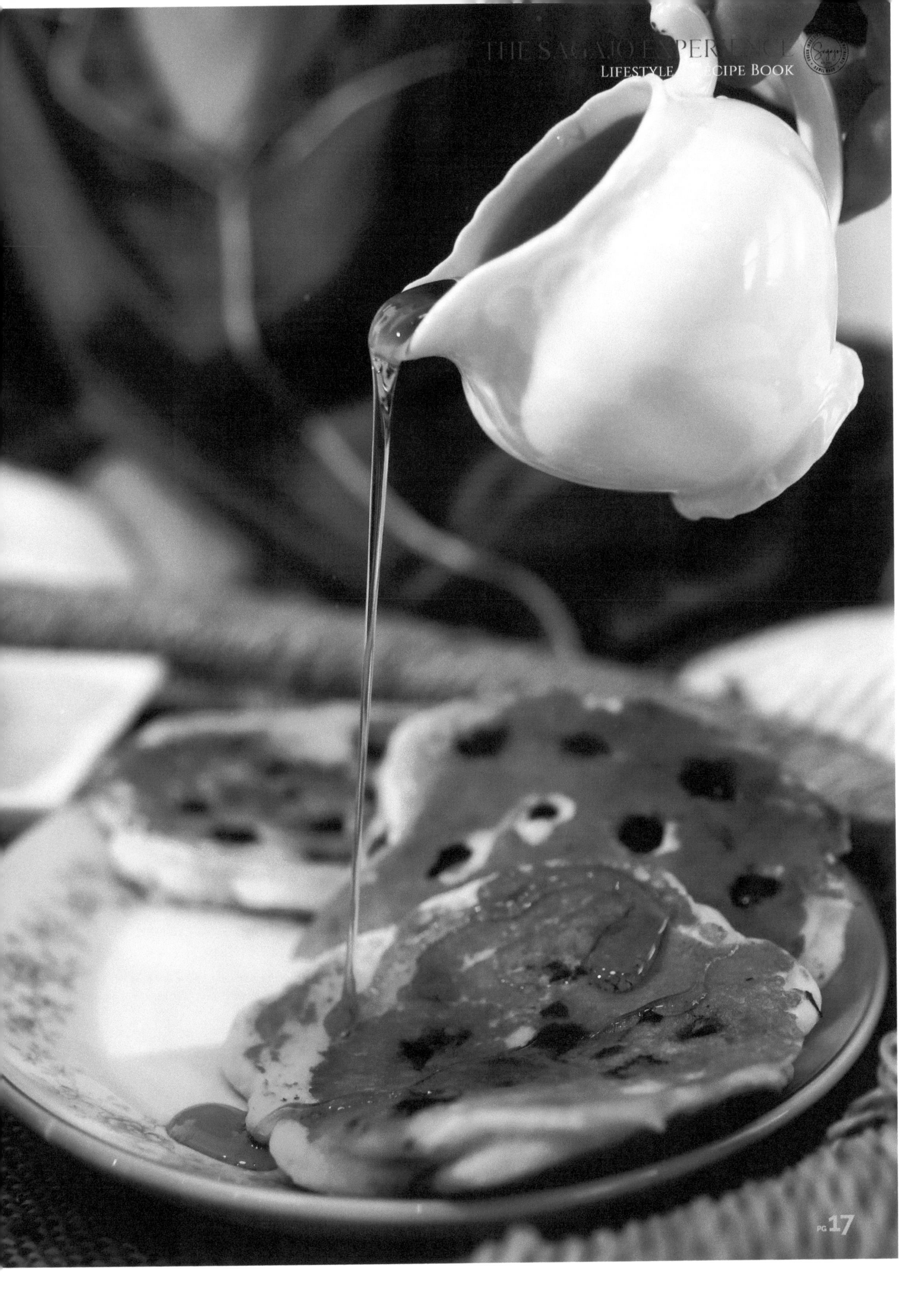

Buttermilk Biscuits Topped with Caramelized Onions

Prep time: 15 minutes
Baking Time: 12-15 minutes
Oven temperature: 350°-or adjusted to your oven

2 cups all-purpose flour
1 tablespoon baking powder
¾ teaspoon salt
½ teaspoon baking soda
5 tbsp chilled butter or vegetable shortening
1 ¼ cup buttermilk

METHOD:

- Preheat the oven to 350°F. In a mixer or large bowl, sift together flour, baking powder, salt, and baking soda.

- Cut the chilled butter/shortening into cubes, and add to the flour. Mix until coarse crumbs form.

- Add the butter milk slowly until a sticky dough forms.

- Turn the dough onto a lightly floured surface. Gather into a disc, kneading very lightly just until everything is smooth.

- Pat the dough or use a rolling pin if necessary to get the dough to about ¾ inch thick. Using a biscuit cutter or a glass dipped in flour, cut the biscuits out, place them two inches apart on an ungreased baking sheet. Gather dough trimmings, pat to ¾ inch thick, and cut out more biscuits.

- Bake the biscuits for 12-15 minutes. Top them with your caramelized onions and serve hot!

Caramelized Onions:

1 large yellow onion
1-2 tbsp of vegetable or olive oil
1 ½ tbsp sugar
½ tsp salt
1 tbsp of apple cider vinegar
¼ of a jalapeno pepper (use more pepper if desired)

METHOD:

- Peel and slice onion thinly.

- Add the oil to a saute pan or a non-stick pan, toss the oni in the oil and add the sugar, salt, and apple cider vinegar.

- Stir to incorporate, and leave them on medium to low hea so they will caramelize.

- Stir again when they are light golden brown, then add the jalapeno peppers and stir.

- Leave them for a little while, but keep watching carefully that they do not BURN! The finished onions should be de golden brown and sweet, so you have to keep stirring and not leave them on their own. Onions burn easily.

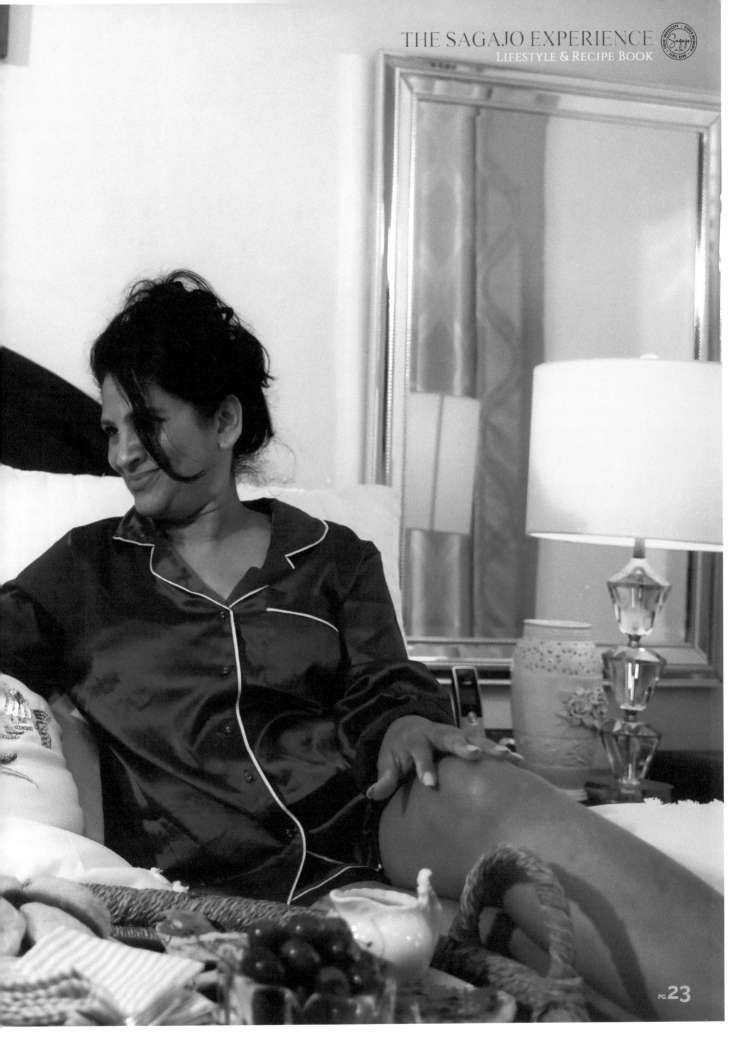

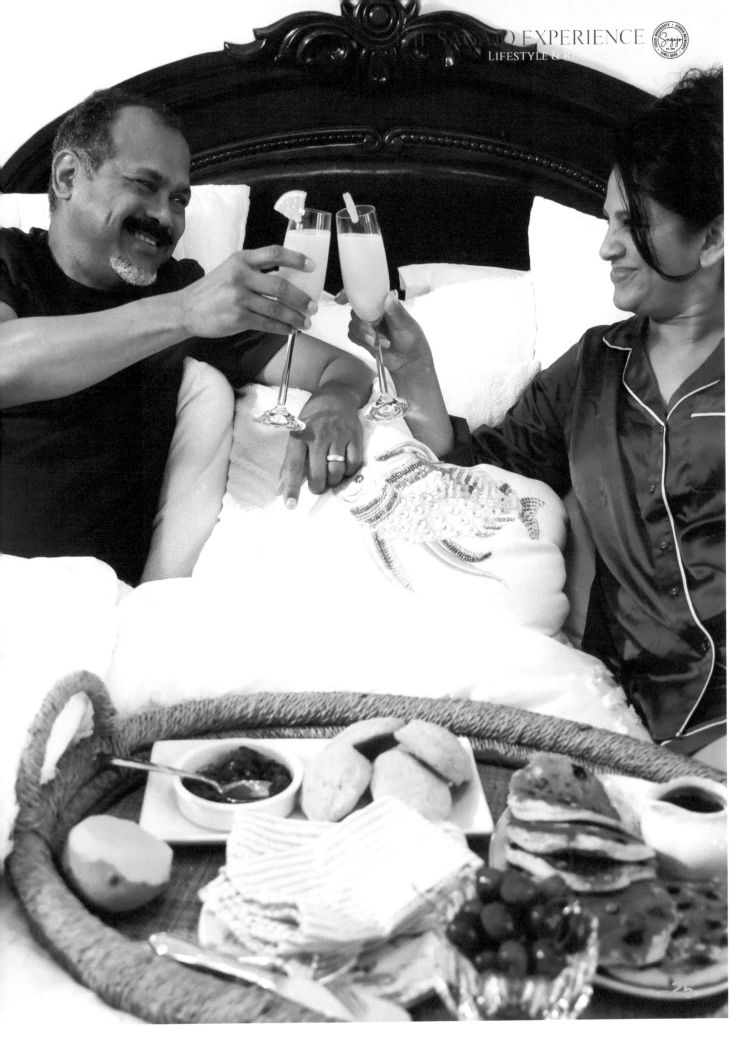

Brunch with my Daughters

Some of my life's happiest and most enjoyable moments are spent with my beautiful daughters and granddaughter. My favourite way to start off the day is gathering for brunch and chatting. These memories touch my heart, most of all because my young ladies all help in deciding the menu and preparing the items.

The Sagajo brunch takes déjeuner à la fourchette to the next level of entertainment. I select a combination of both sweet and savoury dishes like my favourite vegetable quiche with it's flaky and tender crust filled with mushrooms, caramelized onions and asparagus. In addition to this, sweet slices of pumpkin bread, orange poppyseed muffins, and an assortment of fresh seasonal fruit are set out in a glass dish for a colourful presentation.

For beverages I offer a choice of champagne, mimosas, juices, and cappuccino. Since this is not a fancy or formal setting I would choose the kitchen table, island or outdoors to set out plates with a touch of color! Napkins and cutlery, a few potted flowering plants or herbs such as lavender, or rosemary give the space aromatics and beauty. I love putting the food in platters, cake plates and baskets of different heights and shapes to enhance the overall table-scape.

I leave my granddaughter in charge of putting out the napkins and silverware, which she proudly undertakes with a smile. My daughters help with plates and arrange the platters around the table. We grab our drinks and cheers- it's going to be a good day.

In the illustrations here I have chosen the stunning outdoor setting for the healthy fresh air, light and the reflective beauty of the lake. The place settings are well-suited to this informal dining experience: colorful plates, napkins and cutlery enhance the mouth-watering colors of the meal that is laid out on them. Bright white platters and straw baskets of different tones and sizes add a rustic touch to the outdoor setting.

Pumpkin Bread

Preparation time: 20 minutes
Baking time: 20-25 minutes

For the bread:
2 ⅓ cups flour
2 teaspoons baking powder
1 teaspoons baking soda
1 teaspoon cinnamon
1 teaspoon allspice
4 eggs at room temperature
1 cup light brown sugar, packed
1 cup granulated sugar
1 cup vegetable oil
2 cups of pumpkin puree
1 teaspoon vanilla

For the cream cheese frosting:
3-4 ounces of room temperature cream cheese
¾ stick of butter
3 teaspoons of vanilla extract
3 cups of confectioners' sugar
Combine together to form frosting.

- Preheat oven to 350°F. Lightly grease and line a loafpan with parchment paper.

- In a mixing bowl, combine eggs, sugar, puree, vanilla and oil.

- Set aside in another mixing bowl, combine flour, baking powder, baking soda, cinnamon and allspice.

- Add the wet ingredients into the dry ingredients and mix.

- Pour into the loaf pan and bake for 20-25 minutes.

- Allow to cool in loaf pan for 10 minutes before removing to cool on rack.

- When completely cooled, frost the bread.(optional)

- Slice and enjoy! You can also serve the bread with the frosting on the side for a sweet spreadable treat!

Vegetable Quiche

Preparation Time: 1hour and a half
Baking Time: 35-40 minutes

For the dough:
3 cups flour
1 teaspoon salt
1 teaspoon granulated sugar
12 tablespoons of butter- chilled and cubed
2 eggs at room temperature
½ cup ice water

- In a bowl add flour, salt and sugar.

- In a separate bowl, gently beat the eggs and water together.

- Add the flour mixture to a food processor and then add butter and begin to pulse a few times until loosely combined. Mixture should resemble sand.

- Add egg mixture to the food processor and pulse until it comes together and forms a ball.

- Turn the dough onto a floured surface, bring together and flatten into a disc.

- Wrap tightly with plastic wrap and refrigerate for at least 30 minutes.

- Dough is ready to use after refrigeration.

- When dough has finished chilling, turn the dough onto a floured surface and roll into a large circle, about 12 inches in diameter- enough to cover your pie or tart dish.

- Cover the dish and gently press the dough into place.

- Cut the excess dough from the edges. (Save the excess dough and freeze for up to 2 weeks)

- Return to the refrigerator for at least 20 minutes.

- Remove the dough and using a fork, dock the dough.

- Preheat oven to 375°F.

- Place parchment paper over the dough and fill with baking beads. Bake for 15 minutes.

- Take the dough out of the oven and remove the parchment paper and baking beads. Return to the oven for another 10-15 minutes or until lightly golden brown.

- Remove from the oven and let it cool for about 10 minutes. You are now ready to add the quiche filling.

Note: Dough can be made ahead of time, frozen and thawed when ready to use.

For the filling:
3-4 large eggs at room temperature
1/2 cup heavy cream
8oz of Baby Bell mushrooms sliced
½ large red onion, sliced
½ large sweet white onion, sliced
1 cup of asparagus tips
5-6oz of Gruyere cheese, freshly grated
6 fresh sage leaves, finely chopped (yields 1 tablespoon)
6-8 sprigs of fresh parsley, finely chopped (yields 2 tablespoons)
Kosher salt (to taste)
Ground pepper (to taste)
1 teaspoon of ground nutmeg
Olive oil
Truffle oil (optional)

- In a bowl, whisk the eggs, salt, pepper and nutmeg together. Add the heavy cream and combine.

- Set aside in a saute´ pan over medium heat, add a tablespoon of olive oil and a tablespoon of truffle oil. (Or 2 tablespoons of olive oil).

- Add onions and half of the sage.

- Saute´ for 3 minutes or until onions are slightly softened.

- Add mushrooms and remainder of the sage. Saute´ for another 5-7 minutes or until vegetables are browned and softened but not cooked through entirely.

- Remove from heat and place in a bowl and add ½ tablespoon of parsley. Allow it to cool for 10 minutes.

To assemble:
- Preheat oven to 375°F.

- Sprinkle ½ cup of the cheese at the bottom of the quiche.

- Then add the sauteed vegetables, pour the egg mixture over the vegetables.

- Sprinkle another ⅓ cup of the cheese and arrange the asparagus in a design around the quiche. Add remaining cheese to the top.

- Bake for 35-40 minutes or until quiche is set and the top is a tasty golden brown.

Orange Poppy Seed Muffins

Preperation time: 20 minutes
Baking time: 25-20 minutes
Serves 12

2 ½ cups flour
2 tsp baking powder
¼ tsp baking soda
2 tablespoons poppy seeds
⅓ cup granulated sugar
1 cup orange marmalade
1 cup milk
1 stick melted butter
2 eggs at room temperature
1 teaspoon vanilla extract
1 tablespoon orange zest

- Preheat oven to 300°F and lightly spray muffin tin.

- Sift flour, baking powder and soda into a mixing bowl and add sugar and poppy seeds.

- Mix together and set aside. In a saucepan, add butter, ⅔ cup of orange marmalade and Stir over low heat until well combined.

- Set aside and cool slightly.

- In a separate mixing bowl, whisk together eggs, milk, vanilla and orange zest.

- Pour the milk mixture into the flour mixture, then add the melted butter and marmalade and mix just to combine. Do not over mix.

- Scoop the mixture into muffin tins about ¾ of the way full.

- Bake 25-30 minutes or until golden brown.

- Brush with marmalade mixture while still warm. If marmalade has thickened, add a tablespoon of water to loosen. Enjoy warm or room temperature. Store in airtight container.

Apricot and Candied Ginger Scones

Preparation time: 20 minutes Baking time: 25- 30 minutes
Serves 10-12

For the scones:

2 ½ cups of flour
1 tablespoon brown sugar
1 teaspoon baking powder
1 pinch of salt (less than ¼ teaspoon)
4 ozs butter, chilled and cubed
½ cup chopped dried apricots 5 pieces of candied
ginger- chopped
1 tablespoon lemon zest
1 ¼ cup milk, plus extra to brush the top of the scones
1-2 tablespoons turbinado sugar

For the glaze:

2-3 tablespoons of milk
1 cup plus 2 tablespoons confectioners' sugar
1 teaspoon almond extract Whisk together to form
a light glaze

- Preheat oven to 350°F

- Lightly grease or line a baking sheet with baking paper.

- Sift flour, baking powder, and salt in a mixing bowl.

- Add the brown sugar and incorporate.

- Add cubed chilled butter to the flour and mix with the paddle or by hand, until loosely crumbled.

- Add chopped apricots, candied ginger and lemon zest to the mixture.

- Add milk, a little at a time to form a soft sticky dough.

- Turn the dough onto a floured surface and form into a ball. Do not knead.

- Pat the dough into a disc about ¾ inch thick. Use a rolling pin if necessary.

- Using a sharp knife, slice into triangles.

- Transfer to the baking sheet and lay about 1 inch apart.

- Brush with milk and sprinkle with turbinado sugar.

- Bake for 15-20 minutes or until the top begins to brown slightly.

Enjoy warm or at room temperature. Store in an airtight container.

Lunch with My Girlfriends

The times I have my friends come over for lunch are some of the most pleasurable indeed. This occasion is informal so, my kitchen table is a great choice, as I have placed it near a large window that gives a stunning view of the outdoors. I set the table with simple table accessories: woven plate settings, stem-ware, cutlery, napkins and a vase of fresh flowers. I add votives in glass holders to bring warmth and elegance.

There's no way we can have lunch without cocktails! I make a refreshing glass pitcher of my refreshing grapefruit tequila quencher and set it in a tray with glasses rimmed with kosher salt filled with ice ready to top up and toast to our friendship.

I decided on a menu of a delicious crusty bread lightly toasted, drizzled with olive oil and then, sprinkled with parmesan cheese, garlic and parsley to start. For the main course I prepare a delicious Seafood Pasta, which I pair with a bottle of Pinot Grigio that offers the palate a refreshing light crisp note and compliments the piquant pasta flavours. However, if you prefer red, a medium bodied Pinot Noir is also a great choice.

Afterwards we would retire to the living room for a more relaxed space where we continue great conversations over glasses of wine and await dessert. The ideal sweet treat is a decadent Blueberry Lavender pie with its rich & sweet berry flavour that is displayed on a dessert platter. On the coffee table, I've set out small dessert plates, forks and napkins. The prize for finishing a slice of this after lunch? Another glass of wine of course!

Smoked Oysters and Shrimp Chowder

2 sweet onions chopped
2 bay leaves
4-5 garlic cloves chopped
1 ½ tsp fresh thyme
3 carrots peeled and cubed
4 celery stalks cubed
½ fennel cubed (Reserve the fennel stems for garnishing)
1 tsp smoked paprika
8 tbsp of butter
3 russet potatoes cut into cubes
5 tbsp olive oil
8 tbsp of flour
4 cups of clam or vegetable stock
2 cups of heavy cream
1 can of smoked oysters
12 large shrimp cut into pieces
Kosher salt and fresh pepper for tasting

Method:

• In a large pot, add 4 tbsp of butter and olive oil. Add chopped and cubed veggies, thyme & garlic. Sauté until a bit translucent, then add smoked paprika, bay leaves, and cubed potatoes. Sauté this, then add the clam or vegetable stock.

• In a small bowl, add the rest of the butter and flour. Mix into a paste. Add 2 ladles of the hot stock into the flour paste, then add to the pot. Stir in the heavy cream, salt and freshly ground pepper to season and taste, and cook the potatoes until the chowder thickens.

• Season the shrimp with salt and pepper, then add to the chowder along with the drained smoked oysters. Stir for 8 minutes, then remove from the heat. Taste chowder to determine if additional salt and pepper is needed. Serve up and add the fennel stems to decorate the chowder. Enjoy with crusty bread or oyster crackers.

Seafood Pasta

1 large onion chopped
4 tbsp garlic chopped
½ tsp red pepper flakes (optional)
1 ½ tsp tomato paste
1 can of san marzan tomatoes (purée)
1 cup white wine
1 whole lemon, 1 lemon zest and juice (2 lemons)
2 tbsp butter
6 tbsp olive oil
Kosher salt (to taste)
Fresh ground pepper (to taste)
1 box linguine or spaghetti pasta
½ pound shrimp cleaned and de-veined
½ pound sea scallops cleaned
½ pound of mussels, scrubbed, de-bearded
2-3 tbsp parsley chopped

Method:

- In a large pot heat 2 tbsp olive oil on medium high heat. Add 3 tbsp onion and sauté, then add 1 tbsp chopped garlic, and mix well. Add the pepper flakes and tomato paste and sauté for 1 minute. Add the tomato purée and simmer. Add salt and pepper to season and taste, then simmer for 8-12 minutes on low heat.

- In another large pot, boil about 6 quarts of water. Add salt, making sure the water tastes salty. Cook your pasta for about 8 minutes, then drain, but reserve some of your pasta water.

- In a large saucepan heat 2 tbsp olive oil in medium heat. Season the sea scallops with salt and fresh ground peppe Add them to the saucepan and lightly brown on both side for about 1 minute (do not overcook). Take them out and s aside. Season the shrimp. Add the shrimp and sauté until light pink on both sides (do not overcook). Set aside.

- In a large saucepan, heat 2 tbsp of olive oil on medium he then add 2 tbsp of chopped onions and sauté for 1 minute then add 2 tbsp of garlic. Add the lemon zest and add lemon juice and sauté. Add salt and pepper to taste. Add the mussels first & then, the white wine and cover for abou two minutes. Add the butter and toss lightly.
Lastly, add your pasta and a ½ cup of pasta water to the sauce. Add all other ingredients and toss. Then, taste for seasoning.

- Serve this dish on a beautiful platter with lemon wedges and sprinkled parsley.

Blueberry Lavender Pie

Dough:
2 ½ cups all-purpose flour
1 Tbsp Sugar (superfine white sugar)
1 tsp salt
2 Tbsp vegetable oil
1 tbsp of water
2 sticks of cold butter cubed
2 ½ tbsp of corn starch
¼ cup ice cold water
2 tsp white vinegar or lemon juice

Blueberry Lavender Filling:
4 ½ cups fresh blueberries
1 cup of fine white sugar
1 tbsp lemon zest & juice
1 tsp cinnamon
1 tsp culinary lavender

Dough:

- Add the flour, sugar, and salt to a bowl. Add the vegetable oil and combine the ingredients.

- Add the cubed butter, using a pastry cutter or your hands to blend them together until the mixture looks like peas, but not too thoroughly. Some chunks of butter should be visible.

- Add the cold water and the vinegar. Use a wooden spoon to mix, then turn onto a wooden board or work surface. Bring the dough together by folding it over a few times until it forms a ball. Then divide the dough into two pieces.

- Shape into two discs, wrap with plastic wrap and refrigerate for about 2 hours or more.

- Take the dough out of the refrigerator to your work surface. Sprinkle with some flour, roll the bottom layer a little wider than your pie dish, and add to your pie dish, making sure it goes over the dish.

Blueberry Lavender Filling:

Add all ingredients to a saucepan and cook over low heat. A 2 ½ tbsp cornstarch to about 1 tbsp of cold water, stir into y berry filling until it gets thick. After it is cooked, remove it fro the heat, put it into a bowl, and add plastic wrap, touching t berries to make sure there are no air bubbles. Set aside unt room temperature before filling your pie.

To create the Lattice Top Crust:

- Sprinkle flour on your work surface. Shape the dough into square, and roll it a little bit thinner than your bottom crus

- Use a knife or pastry cutter. You should cut strips ½ inch, about 18 pieces.

- Set 8 strips in one direction and every other strip pull backward halfway down the pie, then alternate and repea until you have a lattice pattern. Make sure to trim off all th excess dough.

- Use an egg wash (water and egg) to glaze over the pie, making sure to get all the strips. This helps to ensure a golden crust.

- Bake in oven at 400 °F for 10 mins. Then, turn the temperatu to 375°F for about 40 mins or until golden brown.

- When your pie is finished baking remove it from the oven and let it cool completely. You can serve fresh from the oven, or refrigerate and serve another day.

Grapefruit Quencher

Ingredients:
2 ½ cups of freshly squeezed red grapefruit juice
8-10 tbsp freshly squeezed lime juice
2 dashes of Angostura bitters
2 cups of good tequila
½ cup of agave or simple syrup
2 cups club soda
1-2 red grapefruit cut into wedges for garnishing

In a glass pitcher, add your freshly squeezed red grapefruit juice, lime juice, agave syrup, or simple syrup and stir together. Add the tequila and stir. Top up with club soda and serve with ice in your glasses and grapefruit wedges for garnish.

Simple Syrup Method:
1 ½ cups white sugar
1 ½ cups water

Combine sugar and water in a saucepan over medium-high heat. Stir constantly. Simmer until sugar is dissolved. Let it cool and add it to a bottle and refrigerate for up to 4 weeks. You can use this for your favorite cocktails.

apas with Friends

ve having my friends over to my house, but I don't always
ve time to set-up a formal table. Sometimes, creating a fun
ormal atmosphere with small bites and cocktails is the
rfect way to enjoy great food and even better conversation
people can snack without having to organise utensils and
her fussy bits.

ease note though that informal does not mean sans
biance. Whether it's the kitchen, patio or pillow seats on
living room floor, a relaxed and chic set-up will make it
experience your friends won't soon forget.

favourite place to set-up is the kitchen. On my kitchen
and, I stack plates, bowls and cutlery in vases. Next to that, I
ace a tray of clear crystal stem-ware. Blue linen napkins are a
autiful eye-catching contrast to my dark blue plates. I scatter
election of wine bottles between the tapas platters to help
friends pair the perfect bites. To decorate, I keep it simple
h a bowl of lemons and a bouquet of my favourite flowers. To
ighten your setting, select an Orchid; if you prefer everything
eye-level, a short round vase of Hydrangeas.

lay out the tapas I vary the colors and sizes of the boards and
shware that I use, which would also encourage the creativity
my guests as they select their own combinations. After all,
eat with our eyes. For my Chorizo, Cantaloupe & Artichoke
lad, I select a long rectangular white plate. A bright blue bowl
a cutting board is best suited for the Eggplant Dip with slices
my Crusty Bread. The centerpiece for this fun and festive
t-up is a large sparkling pitcher of my refreshing Blackberry
sil Smash

Eggplant Dip

This can be served up before serving your meals.
*Using crusty bread recipe to serve up

2 large eggplants
1 medium onion - finely chopped
2 red bell peppers
5 tbsp of good extra virgin olive oil
4 garlic cloves - finely chopped
½ lemon zest and juice
2 tablespoon of cilantro
1 tsp cumin
1 tsp smoked paprika
Kosher salt and pepper taste

- Peel the skin off the eggplant and cut into cubes.

- Heat the oil in the saucepan. Add the onions and garlic, and sauté for 3 minutes. Then add the eggplant and sauté for 6-8 minutes. Add the bell peppers, cumin, smoked paprika, lemon juice and zest. Season with Kosher salt and pepper to taste continue to cook until soft, making sure to break down any chunks of eggplant.

- Sprinkle with chopped cilantro and serve in a beautiful dish alongside some crusty bread for spreading or dipping.

Crusty Bread

(No knead recipe)
Bake at 450°F
You will need a Dutch oven

3 cups all purpose flour
¾ tsp yeast (you can use instant yeast)
2 tsp sugar
1 ¼ tsp salt
1 ¼ cup water

- In a large bowl, add the flour, yeast, sugar, salt, stir together with a whisk. Add lukewarm water and stir with a wooden spoon or dough whisk. The dough should look a little shaggy. Cover with plastic wrap and let rise in warm place for 2 hours until double in size.

- Pre heat the oven to 450°F. Place the Dutch oven into the oven to get hot.

- Transfer the dough onto a floured surface and dust the top of the dough with some flour. Use a bench scraper to fold dough onto itself to form a ball.

- Place the ball of dough into a shallow bowl with parchment paper, cover with plastic film and let the dough rise for about 35 minutes or until it doubles in size.

- After the dough rises, use a knife with a little oil on it (so that the dough will not stick to the knife) to score the dough. Cut into the centre of dough with the oiled knife, making sure to slice into it.

- Carefully remove the Dutch oven using mittens, remove the cover and transfer the dough with parchment paper into the hot Dutch oven, close with the lid and bake for 30 minutes with lid on. Then remove the lid, reduce the heat to 400 and bake for about 8-12 minutes, until its golden and crusty.

- Remove it from the Dutch oven, and let cool for a few minutes. You can hear the bread crackling. This bread is wonderful with soups or salads, it's very delicious and nutritious.

Burrata, Melon and Prosciutto Salad

1 or 2 fresh packs of Baby Arugula
1 Burrata ball
3 thin slices of honeydew melon
3 thin slices of cantaloupe melon
8-10 slices of prosciutto
1 - 2 pinches of kosher salt
3 tbsp good extra virgin olive oil
Drizzle of balsamic glaze

- On a large plate or platter arrange the Baby Arugula around the perimeter, leaving the centre clear.

- Peel the Honeydew melon and slice three thin slices. Do the same with the cantaloupe.

- Arrange the slices of honeydew melon first, then add the cantaloupe slices, making sure to show the slices from both melons.

- Add the Burrata Ball in the centre on top of the thinly sliced melons. With a spoon, mash the Burrata, then pile on the slices of prosciutto onto the Burrata ball, arranging to give the centre some height, until you have a beautiful circular salad.

- Sprinkle the salt onto the entire salad. Pour the extra virgin olive oil all over the salad, then drizzle the balsamic glaze over everything to complete the salad for serving.

This beautiful salad can be served as a first course to your lunch or dinner.

Beet Salad with Vegetables

2 red beets
2 large carrots, peeled, and cut into cubes
2 large potatoes - Yukon gold - peeled and cut into cubes
1/2 of red onion, diced
1 can of pink beans - pinto or Roman
1/2 cup of cilantro chopped
1/2 cup fresh dill chopped
1 tsp kosher salt (to your taste)
1/2 tsp of freshly ground pink peppercorns (to your taste)
1/2 tsp lemon zest
4 tbsp of sunflower oil
1/4 cup of apple cider vinegar
2 tbsp of sugar

Vinaigrette:

To a mason jar add Apple Cider vinegar, sugar, sunflower oil, lemon zest, a few pinches of kosher salt, and freshly ground pink peppercorns. Give the jar a good shake to combine the ingredients.

Salad:

- Remove the green stems and wash beets thoroughly, removing any dirt. Add beets to a pot and bring water to a boil, lower to a simmer. Cook the beets for about 45 minutes or until you can pierce through with a knife and they are tender. Drain and cool the beets, remove the skins and cut beets into about 1/2 inch cubes.

- Place the potatoes and carrots into a deep pot, add salt and bring to a boil, lower to simmer, and cook potatoes and carrots until just fork tender. Avoid overcooking them. Drain and cool, then cut into cubes.

- In a large bowl, add the cubed beets, potatoes, carrots, beans, red onions, chopped herbs, give a toss, then add your vinaigrette and toss to combine. Taste before adding more salt or pepper if you desire.

- This salad is beautiful and can be served at room temperature or made ahead a day before, and can last up to 5 days refrigerated.

Shrimp Salad with Mango and Cucumber

1 ½ cups of white wine
1 ½ lb of shrimp/prawns (medium, peeled, and deveined)
1 large ripe mango
1 cucumber peeled
3-4 cups lettuces (mixed, torn in pieces)
2-3 tbsp fresh basil

Vinaigrette:

½ cup olive oil
Zest of 1 lemon
2 tbsp of lemon juice
½ tsp kosher salt
1 tbsp honey
½ tsp brown sugar
¼ tsp red pepper flakes
1 tsp dill finely chopped
¼ pinch cayenne pepper

Add all ingredients to a mason jar or bowl. Mix or whisk together.

Method:

· In a saucepan over high heat bring the wine to a boil. Add the shrimp/ prawns and cook just until they turn pink - about 3-5 minutes. Remove and add to a bowl, then refrigerate.

· Peel the mango and cut out all the flesh from the seed, then dice the pieces. Peel the skin off the cucumber, divide and slice into small cubes.

· In a large bowl, combine the torn lettuce and basil. Drizzle vinaigrette over lettuce and mix well.

· Drizzle a few tablespoons of vinaigrette on the shrimp, toss and let stand for 5 minutes.

· Add lettuce to your desired platter or individual plates. Top off with mango and cucumbers. Distribute the remaining vinaigrette.

· Sprinkle with dill and serve.

Melon, Artichoke and Chorizo Tapas

7 ounces of a good Chorizo Sausage (Remove the casing)
12-14 globe artichokes (you can use canned or bottled artichokes)
1 lemon-juice and zest
5 tbsp of good olive oil
1 medium size cantaloup (cut into bite sized cubes)
4 sprigs of tarragon
1 tsp of mustard
1 tbsp of champagne vinegar
Salt and pepper to taste

Method:

- To prepare the dressing, add all the ingredients into a medium bowl and whisk them together.

- Peel the melon, cut into halves and scoop out the seeds. Cut the melon into cubes.

  - After removing the casing from the Chorizo sausage, cut into bite-sized cubes. Add to the cubed melon.

- If using canned or bottled artichokes, remove them from the can/bottle, drain them from the marinate, and cut them into halves.

- Pour the dressing over the melon, Chorizo and artichokes and toss together, garnish with the chopped tarragon, and serve up to your guests. Makes great tapas. It can be served with a great bottle of red or white wine.

Dinner with my Family

Sagajo Dining is all about creating settings and menus that draw loved ones together to share a joyful meal experience. For me, the most memorable are those with my family. Whether it's holiday celebrations, birthdays, anniversaries or formal Sunday dinners, I add my special touches to create a warm yet elegant atmosphere for everyone's enjoyment!

When food brings family members together, the menu should be something special, with courses of items that delight everyone. I am suggesting for this particular menu my family's favorites, such as Herb-roasted Rack of Lamb and Mustard Honey Glazed Cornish Hens. Whenever any of these grace the table, it brings us together for fun, laughter and love, so why not splurge when making meals for the people you love? Enjoyment also comes when my family helps in the kitchen. My daughters and I like to chat while preparing the food, and laughter rings out in the kitchen especially when the girls make funny comments like "Don't forget to sprinkle some parsley on that before mom sees it."

There's that moment I long for when I look around the dinner table and see happy smiles as we gather to pray, eat and enjoy an exquisite meal with all its trimmings. Usually it's accompanied by an array of creative descriptions from my granddaughter like, "Is yummilicious Yamma!" No food critic could ever top that comment.

Mustard and Honey Glazed Cornish Hens

6 Cornish hens
1 tsp smoked paprika
½ cup honey
3-4 tbsp Dijon Mustard
1 tbsp Apple Cider Vinegar
½ tsp kosher salt & fresh black
pepper to taste
2 tbsp of olive oil
Parchment paper

- Using a sharp knife or kitchen scissors, remove the back and neck bones of hens and butterfly. Press down on the breast bone to flatten them.

- Combine the paprika, Apple Cider Vinegar, mustard, honey, and massage half of the mixture evenly over the hens. Let marinate at room temperature for 1 hour, or you can refrigerate the hens for up to 8-10 hours. Reserve the remaining mixture for basting the hens while baking.

- In a heavy skillet heat the oil and add the hens, searing them lightly. Then, put them on a tray lined with parchment paper and put them into a 375°F oven. Bake until golden brown and,
  with the remaining mixture, glaze them when they are finished.

- Note: Be careful not to overcook the hens, they are delicate.

- Serve with roasted potatoes or your favorite sides.

Herb Roasted Rack of Lamb with Lavender

1 rack of lamb
2 cloves garlic chopped plus 6 whole garlic cloves
4 sprigs of rosemary chopped plus four whole sprigs
(for garnish)
1 tbsp of French blue culinary lavender
1 tbsp of kosher salt (to taste)
1 tsp of freshly ground pepper (to taste)
4 tbsp olive oil

- First, trim any excess fat off the lamb and pat dry with paper towels. Brush the lamb with olive oil. Rub chopped garlic, rosemary, French lavender, kosher salt, and pepper thoroughly covering the meat.

- Heat a few tbsp of olive oil in a large heavy skillet. Add the whole garlic cloves and sauté for about 1 minute, remove and set aside. Sear the rack of lamb on medium- high heat for about 2 minutes per side until brown on both sides. Transfer the lamb rack into a roasting pan, place into the oven at 425°F and roast for about 8-12 minutes, use a meat thermometer to check for the medium-rare setting, which is about 145°F.

- Remove the rack of lamb from the oven before it reaches the internal temperature as it will continue to cook after it's removed from the oven. The internal temperature will continue to rise about 10 degrees upon standing.

- Let the rack of lamb rest for about 5 minutes before slicing. The resting process ensures the juices will not run out when You slice into the rack of lamb.

- Serve on a platter garnished with the garlic cloves that you sautéed earlier, and the fresh rosemary sprigs, and enjoy.

Side dish: Mediterranean Potatoes

4 tbsp olive oil
2 lbs baby potatoes cut into halves
1 shallot thinly sliced
3 garlic gloves finely minced
12 kalamata olives
12 frespatrano olives cut into halves
3 roasted peppers; julienne
20 cherry tomatoes
½ cup white wine

Method:

- Heat 4 tbsp of olive oil in a saucepan on high heat, then add potatoes and sauté for about 3 minutes.

- Add shallots, garlic, olives, bell pepper and tomatoes on medium high heat. Sauté for 2-3 minutes then de-glaze with the ½ cup white wine for 1-2 minutes.

- Cover for 1-2 mins (until the potatoes are fork tender).

- Season with salt and pepper.

- Garnish with chopped fresh parsley or any of your favorite herbs.

Roasted Brussels Sprouts and Butternut Squash

25 -30 Brussels sprouts cut into halves
1 butternut squash cut into cubes
6 tbsp olive oil
2 tbsp honey
1 tbsp of aged balsamic vinegar
2 tbsp kosher salt
1 tsp fresh ground pepper
1 head of roasted garlic
1 small red sweet pepper thinly sliced into circles (optional for garnish)
Few chopped parsley leaves (optional for garnish)
Fennel prawns (optional for garnish)

Bake at 450°F: 25 - 35 minutes or until browned

2 large bowls
2 sheet pans lined with parchment paper

- Peel and cut butternut squash into cubes, add to a bowl, toss 3 tbsp olive oil with kosher salt and freshly ground pepper. Add to the prepared sheet pan and put into the oven. Bake until lightly browned and thoroughly cooked.

- Wash the Brussels sprouts, trim the bottoms off, then cut into halves. Add to a large bowl toss with 3 tbsp olive oil, kosher salt, freshly ground pepper. Add to a prepared sheet pan and bake until it acquires the desired light brown hue.

- Cut the head of garlic in half, sprinkle with kosher salt, fresh ground pepper, drizzle with olive oil and wrap into a piece of foil. Put into the oven for about 25 minutes until soft and light brown in color, remove from oven, set aside to cool.

- Remove roasted butternut squash and roasted Brussels sprouts from the oven. Add them to a large mixing bowl, add honey and aged balsamic, and gently toss to combine.

- Remove roasted garlic from foil, squeeze the roasted garlic cloves into the roasted Brussels sprouts and roasted butternut squash and give a toss to combine.

- Serve on a platter of your choice, using the thinly sliced red sweet peppers, chopped parsley, and fennel for a colorful garnish.

athering for Special Occasions

the Caribbean, when we refer to "special" meals, we are king about those occasions when we pull out all the stops: ur best dishware and cutlery, the really beautiful decor and ace settings, simply the finest of everything you own for a rmal dining experience with your family and friends. This is mething I set up in my dining room, a space that combines ite `effectively elegance and ease, so adding decor is no erous task.

y dining table is a warm, dark oak, so the neutral table runner its it perfectly.

und place-mats, and cream napkins making sure not to con- al the table's surface too much. Next I lay down silver plate argers for the fine China plate settings, silver cutlery and m-ware. The colors of the water goblets, would be light ue, gentle gold or even a dusty rose to add a hint of sparkle.

r the floral arrangements, I would choose fresh cut flowers d set them into either one large centerpiece, or distribute ller flowers in a few decorative vases. Remember- this where u can select your favorites but I prefer Hydrangeas, Peonies, ses and Lilies. Candles are a must as candlelight adds a mantic feel with its soft glowing flickering light! Ambient strumental music with a soft tone is perfect as it does not own out great conversations. This is very important because sets the overall atmosphere that you're creating for your uests to feel special and comfortable.

ice the ambiance is set I return to my menu by making a list what I will be preparing to serve my guests. Planning ahead iables me to create a well thought out menu that I can easily air with wines. While I am not a Sommelier, my experience a chef has given me the opportunity to understand the mplexities of wine pairing. If you know your food, you'll iow your wine...and I know my food.

Beef Brisket

Serves 8-12

1 Brisket of beef
2 tbsp of Kosher Salt
½ cup sugar
1 ½ tsp ground ginger
1 ½ tsp ground coriander
1 tsp clove
1 tsp nutmeg
1 tsp ground all spice
2 ½ tbsp of freshly ground pepper
8 tbsp olive oil
4 celery stalks chopped
3 sweet onions chopped
2 ½ cups of beef stock
2 cups tomato purée
½ cup chopped parsley for garnishing

Glazed Carrots with Raisins
(to accompany the Brisket)

12-15 Carrots peeled and cut into ¼ inch slices or dices.
1 ½ cups of golden raisins
2 whole sweet onions sliced thinly
½ cup of white wine
1 cup of chicken stock
1 tbsp orange zest and the juice
5 tbsp of olive oil
1 tbsp of Apple Cider Vinegar
5-6 tbsp of honey
Kosher salt and fresh ground pepper to taste

Method for the Brisket

• In a large glass container or dish with a cover, place the brisket. Then combine the first seven ingredients, mix well and rub all over the both sides of the brisket. Cover and refrigerate for twenty-four hours. After the meat has been marinated remove it and pat it dry. Add the Kosher salt and freshly ground pepper.

• In a large and wide dish or heavy pot heat 4 tbsp of oil and brown the brisket on both sides. Then remove the brisket, and add the rest of the oil to the pot. Add the onions and celery, and sauté the mixture until it's a bit tender and translucent, which should take about 8-10 minutes.

• Place the brisket back into the deep dish/pot, making sure to add some of the onions on the top of the brisket, cover and reduce the heat. Simmer for about 1 ½ hours, then add the beef stock and tomato purée and cook 1 ½ hours or until the meat is tender.

• For carving, remove the brisket and let it rest covered with for about fifteen minutes. Finish simmering the onions and juices over a medium heat. Add salt and pepper to taste for seasoning. Slice the brisket and place it into a beautiful serving dish. Add the pan juices on top of the brisket. Sprinkle with chopped parsley for presentation. Serve and enjoy!

Glazed Carrots with Raisins

• In a saucepan heat the olive oil, add the onions and cook until tender, then add the   carrots, orange zest and juice.

• After this, add the golden raisins, sauté, then add honey, wine stock, and apple cider vinegar and stir, bring to a boil, then reduce to a simmer until carrots are tender. This should take about 10 minutes.

• Finally, season with Kosher salt and pepper to taste. Serve alongside your Brisket.

Basmati Rice Pilaf

2 tbsp of olive oil
1 tbsp chopped ginger (finely chopped)
2 carrots (peel the skin off and diced)
1 cinnamon stick
1⁄2 of sweet onion, diced
1 cup of fragrant Basmati rice
2 cups chicken stock or vegetable stock
2 tbsp of dried cranberries
2 tbsp cilantro (chopped)
1⁄2 tsp kosher salt (to taste)

- In a saucepan over medium heat, heat the olive oil and add diced carrots, diced onions, ginger, and cinnamon stick.

- Sauté the mixture until it is a bit translucent for five minutes. Make sure not to overcook.

- Add the Basmati rice and Sauté for three minutes.

- Add chicken or vegetable stock. Add salt to taste, bring to a boil, for about two minutes, then reduce the heat and cover. Allow to simmer for fifteen minutes, until all the liquid is absorbed.

- Add your cranberries, and remove the saucepan from the heat.

- After six minutes add the chopped cilantro and mix together, fluffing the mixture with a fork.

- Serve in a clear glass bowl or simple decorative plate

Whole Roasted Red Snapper

Bake @ 350°F 30-35 minutes

2 ½ lbs of whole red snapper
2 tbsp ginger chopped
4-5 sprigs of Rosemary
5 sprigs of thyme
2 tbsp chopped cilantro
2 lemon slices-(plus 1 more whole lemon for decoration)
1 whole garlic bulb, plus 5 garlic glove sliced
1 tbsp of smoked paprika
1 red bell pepper and 1 yellow bell pepper
Kosher salt and fresh ground pepper (to season and taste)
1 large sweet onion
¼ cup olive oil
Butcher's twine

- Thoroughly remove the scales from the snapper; and clean and rinse the cavity.

- Pat dry the fish. Then, using a sharp knife, score the fish by making 4 slashes on both sides. Add 2 tbsp of olive oil and rub onto both sides, season generously with Kosher salt, smoked paprika and fresh ground pepper, making sure to get the inside of the fish cavity and in between the slashes.

- Stuff the Rosemary Sprigs, thyme sprigs, lemon slices, garlic slices and ginger into the cavity of the fish. Using the butcher's twine, make 3 separate ties to hold the fish together.

- Place the fish on a baking tray or dish coated with olive oil. Bake for 30 minutes, then put the oven on broil and broil the fish just until it has a bit more colour on it before removing it from the heat.

- In a saucepan, heat some olive oil then add the julienne yellow and red bell peppers slices and the sliced onions. Sauté for 2 minutes, then add salt and pepper to taste.

- To serve, add your roasted whole red snapper to a large serving platter or dish. Decorate the top with some lemon slices. Add the sautéed onion and bell peppers to both sides of the fish. Add the rest of the rosemary sprigs and sprinkle with the chopped cilantro.

Roasted Duck with Crispy Roasted Potatoes

Serves 6-8
Pre heat oven 500°F 7-10 mins
Then bring down to 300°F for 1 hour and a half

2 whole ducks (room temperature with necks removed
and wing-tips tucked under the back of the duck)
8-10 bunches of thyme
8 garlic cloves minced
Zest of 3 large lemons
3 tbsp Kosher salt
2 tbsp freshly ground pepper
2 whole onions
2 bottles of beer

Method:

- Remove the necks of the ducks and tuck the wing tips under the duck.

- Salt the ducks and leave overnight in the refrigerator. Take them out and wash them, pat dry and season generously with Kosher salt and pepper. Make sure to season thoroughly the inside cavity of the ducks. Then add the bundles of thyme, garlic and onions cut into halves or quarters into the cavity of each of the ducks.

- Place the ducks onto the baking trays with wire racks to roast the ducks. Pour the beer all over the ducks and place in the oven, first for 7-15 minutes on 500°F, then lower the heat to 325°F and bake until golden brown (for about 1 1/2 hours) then take them out and let them rest for half of an hour. Return them to the oven to broil for about 4-6 minutes to ensure the skin is crisp.

- Let them rest before cutting them and serving with your favorite side dishes.

Crispy Roasted Potatoes

pot with water for boling russet potatoes
8-10 Russet Potatoes
6-7 tbsp olive oil
4 tbsp Kosher salt
4 Rosemary sprigs
6 thyme sprigs
8 leaves of sage
10 garlic cloves

Bake at 375°F

- Peel the skins off the potatoes and cut them into halves. Parboil them in salted water for about 8-10 minutes, then drain them. Place them on a baking tray. Add the olive oil and Kosher salt, then place in the oven and roast for 30 minutes.

- Remove after 30 minutes. Coat the potatoes with the rest of the olive oil, then add the rosemary, thyme, sage and whole garlic cloves. Return to the oven for 30-35 minutes. They should be deep golden brown, crispy on the outside and tender in the middle when they are done. These crispy potatoes can be served alongside the roasted duck.

Marinated Roasted Spatchcocked Chicken

1 whole chicken
2 bottles of beer
1 sprig of sage
6 whole peppercorns
2 tsp kosher salt (to your taste)
Fresh ground black pepper (to your taste)
2 tsp of ground ginger
1 tsp of herbs de Provence
3-4 tbsp olive oil

Method for Spatchcocked Chicken

- Spatchcock the chicken by removing the backbone with kitchen shears and flatten it by pressing through the breast bone.

- Pour 2 bottles of beer of choice over the chicken, and add a sprig of sage, and 6 whole peppercorns. Let the chicken marinate in the beer for three hours.

- After marinating the chicken, remove and pat dry. Discard the marinade.

- Season the chicken with kosher salt, fresh ground black pepper, ground ginger and herbs de Provence.

- Put the chicken onto a lined baking tray and drizzle with olive oil. Place in the oven heated to 425°F for approximately 55 minutes, until your chicken is a beautiful golden brown.

- Let the chicken rest for about 6 minutes before serving. Serve with roasted sweet potatoes or your favorite side dish.

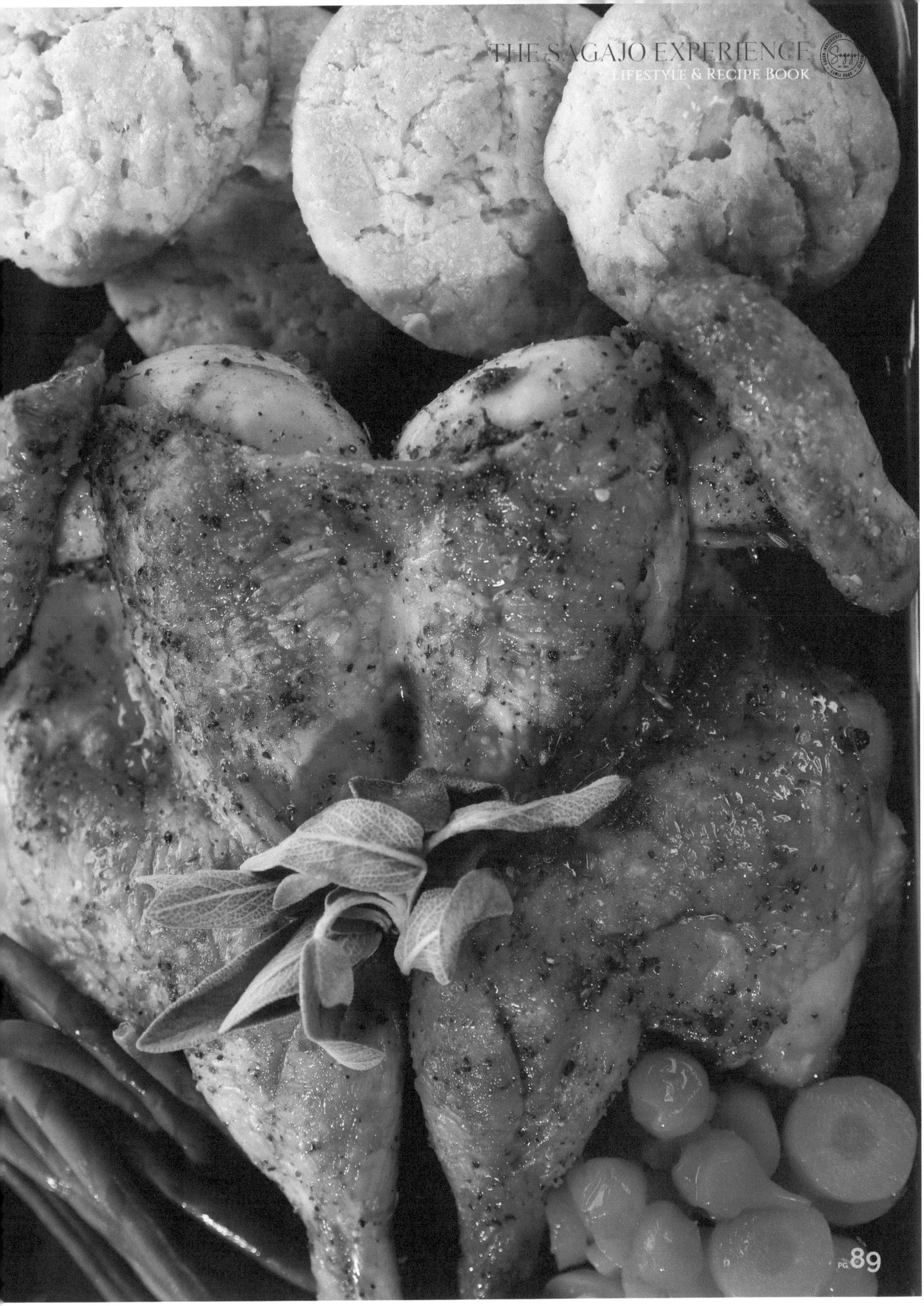

Chef
Debbie Berment
Sagajo

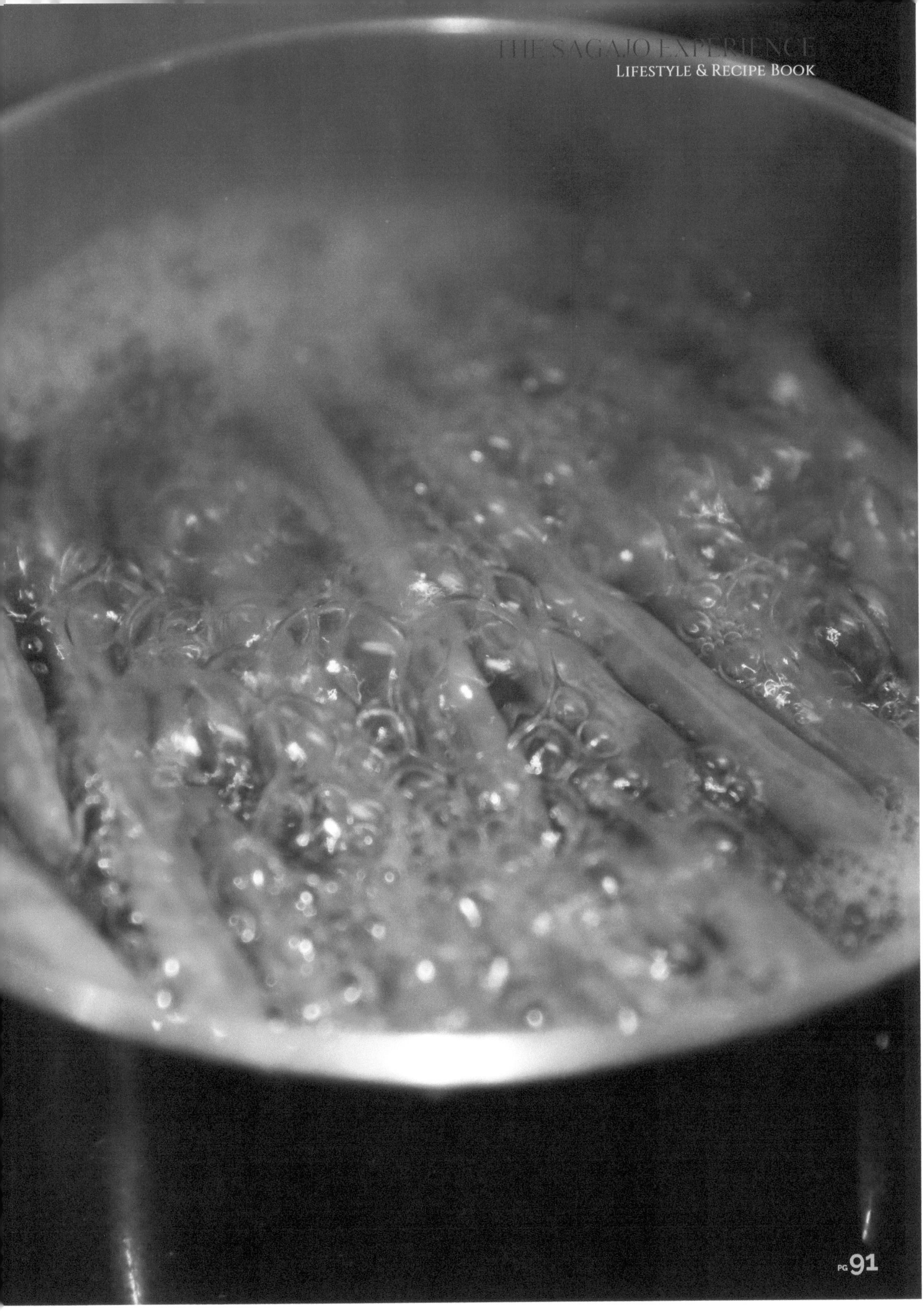

Chilean Sea Bass with lemon butter sauce topped with caviar

2 non-stick pans. 1 for sauce.
4-6 to 8oz of Chilean Sea Bass (your choice on size of fish)
Kosher salt to taste(season generously)
Fresh ground pepper to taste
3 tbsp of olive oil
4 tbsp butter
4 tbsp of caviar (finishing topper)
4 medium baking potatoes thinly sliced (use a mandolin for more precise sizes and better for evenly baking)
2 sprigs fresh thyme
25-30 green beans
4 whole garlic cloves
5 tbsp lemon juice plus 2 whole lemons for slicing and garnishing
¼ cup white wine
1 fennel bulb-(for fennel ferns to garnish)

For the Sea Bass

- On stove top pre-heat non-stick pan on medium high.
- Sear the bass on the stove top for 2-3 minutes on each side until skin side is golden and crisp.
- Finish in the oven temp:400°F for 8-10 minutes making sure that it is skin side up.

Lemon Butter Sauce

1 ½ stick of butter cut into cubes and added to the freezer
1 shallot chopped
5-6 tbsp of freshly squeezed lemon juice
½ cup white wine

- To a saucepan on medium heat add shallots, freshly squeezed lemon juice, and white wine. While the lemon ju and white wine are reducing, take out butter from the free and whisk in the chilled cubes of butter one at a time unti is fully incorporated. Turn off the stove and sprinkle the fennel ferns at the end. Then pour onto your fish when rea to plate and serve.

Potato Slices

- Place in a 400°F oven for about 30mins until lightly golde brown.

- Peel and slice potatoes thinly either using a Mandolin or knife .Add the thinly sliced potatoes to a bowl, season with salt and pepper, drizzly with olive oil.

- Layer the potatoes half way onto each other to a baking t with parchment paper and bake until lightly brown in colo and cooked. Using a spatula take a few of the potatoes an drape onto the fish.

Green Beans

- Blanch for 2-3 minutes

- Trim off the stems from the green beans. Add them to salt boiling water for about 3 minutes, until they are bright gree then take them out and pat dry the green beans; set aside a saucepan on medium heat add 1 tbsp of butter, pinch of salt, add 1 tbsp finely chopped garlic toss the green bean into pan until they are all thoroughly coated. Remove then and set aside for plating.

Plating

- For plating we place the fish in the centre. We then add th green beans at the side, and top with caviar. Finally, add t sauce and then sprinkle with the fennel ferns. Serve to yo guests and enjoy.

SWEETS FOR MY SWEET

weets for my Sweet

e way to bring a special meal to a sublime close is the Sagajo
le dessert menu. One of my favorites, enjoyed by family and
ends alike, is my Red Wine Poached Pears dish, simple, yet
fully delicious. The other favorite is my Buttery Madelaines,
htly dusted with confectioner's sugar and beautifully plated
add a sweet finish to a casual occasion.

urring the summer, I love serving my Mango Lime Pudding
my Mixed Berry Pavlova filled with lucious cream- both
autiful and elegant desserts. My Raspberry Mousse is also an
ticing dessert to serve, whether it's a relaxed lunch, or a
-down dinner with loved ones.

nocolate lovers, I haven't forgotten about you. Serve up my
nocolate Roulaude with Orange Cream filling, It's a slice of
veet indulgence. Sometimes the simplest pumpkin bread
n be sliced thinly and served on an attractive cutting board
r a less formal kitchen gathering. Whatever the occasion may
e- don't forget the sweets for your sweet!

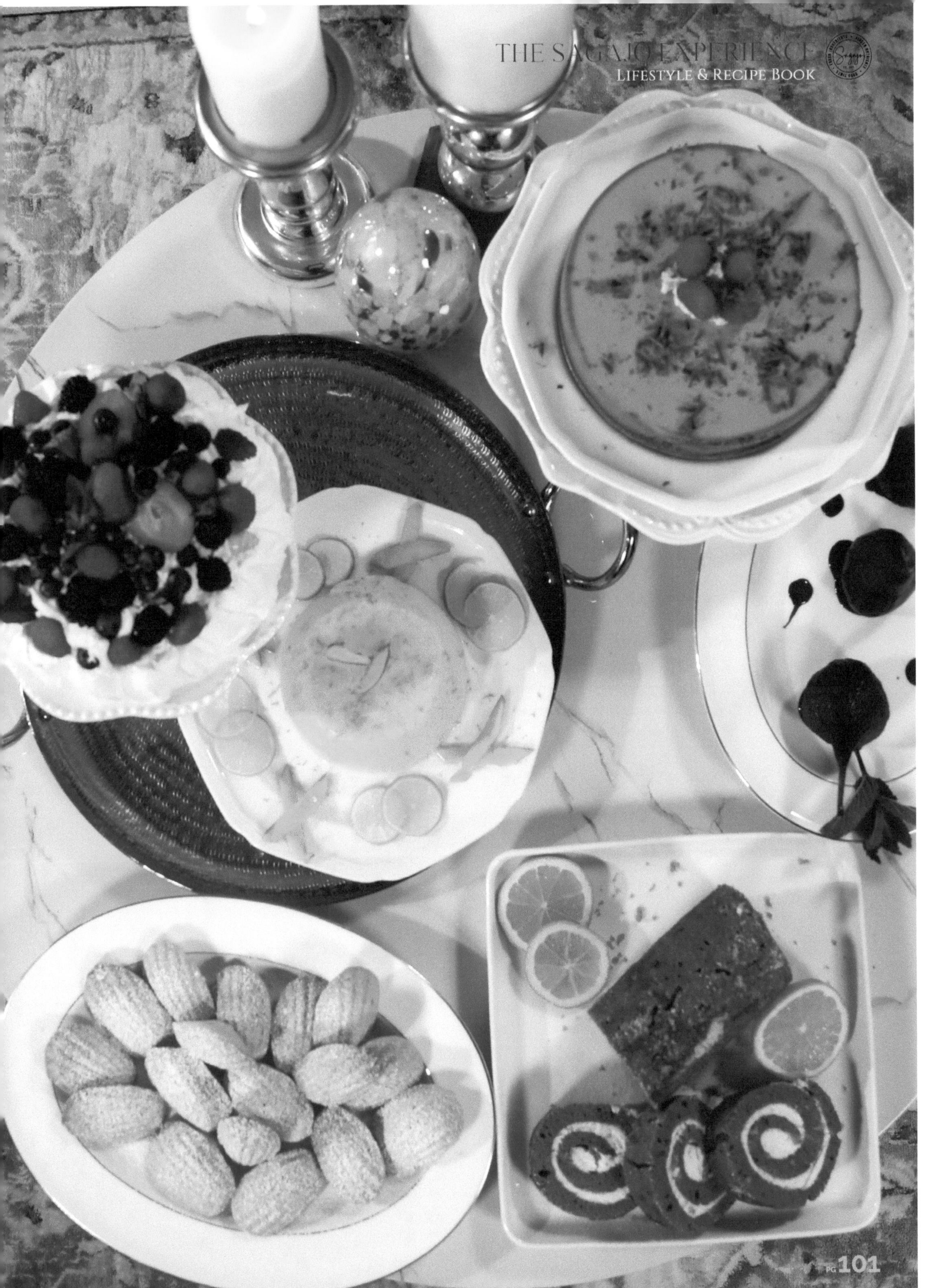

Summer Mango Lime Pudding

2 large ripened mangoes
1 ¼ cups of milk
¼ cup of corn starch
¼ cup of milk
2-3 pinches of salt
Lime juice and zest
Whipped cream

- Peel the mangoes and remove the flesh. Keep some of the pieces for the garnish. Blend the remaining pieces with 1 cup of sugar and 2-3 pinches of salt.

- Add milk and blend into a smooth, thick purée. Transfer the mixture to a pot, set aside.

- In a small dish add corn starch and milk and mix to create a slurry. Set aside.

- Put the pot with blended mango onto the stove on medium heat and stir until it bubbles, then add the slurry, stirring vigorously on low heat until it thickens. Keep stirring to ensure a smooth consistency, let it thicken and bubble.

- Turn off the heat and add the lime juice, then pour this mixture into greased mold, and allow to cool to room temperature. After this, refrigerate for 4 hours, unmold and serve cold. Garnish with mango pieces or whipped cream.

Raspberry Mousse

Oven temp 350°F
Prep time:25-30 mins
Cooking time: 40 mins
Chilling time: 2-4hours before serving

Crust:
1 ½ cups of Graham cracker crumbs
3 tbsp of honey
⅓ cup melted butter

Cookie Layer:
½ cup butter
½ cup sugar (fine white)
2 large eggs
⅓ cup of whole milk
⅓ cup all purpose flour + ½ cup almond flour
2 tsp baking powder

Raspberry Mousse:
2 cups of fresh raspberries
½ cup apple juice
1 tbsp of lemon juice
4 egg yolks
1 ½ packets of gelatin
¼ cup of cold water
⅓ cup sugar
1 cup heavy cream whipped

Prepare the crust (base):
Combine the Graham cracker crumbs, honey and melted butter in a bowl, mix to combine, spread into the greased spring-form pan and set aside.

Prepare the cookie (middle layer):
In a food processor or hand mixer, add the egg yolks and butter and blend together. Add the flour, milk, baking powde and almond flour and mix to combine. Pour the batter into the spring-form pan, bake for 30-35minutes, then cool and refrigerate.

Prepare the mousse (topping):
In a saucepan, add the fresh raspberries, juice of lemon, app juice and sugar and bring to a boil, then turn the heat down t simmer for about 3 minutes before removing from the heat. Add the egg yolks and the gelatin. Then, add the mixture to food processor and purée, then strain and refrigerate for 15 minutes. remove from refrigerator and add the whipped cream, folding it into the raspberries purée; pour it into the spring-form pan and refrigerate for 2-3 hours or longer befor unhinging the pan to remove the mousse.

Garnish/ Decorations
You can use fresh raspberries and/or raspberry whipped cream to top it off.

Chocolate Roulade with Orange Cream Filling

¾ cup cake flour
2 tablespoons of good cocoa powder
¼ cup granulated sugar
+ ¼ cup granulated sugar (for adding to egg whites)
¼ cup of confectioners sugar to cream filling
5 large eggs, separated (separate the egg yolk from the egg whites)

Orange Cream Filling:
1 ¼ Cups of heavy whipping cream
1 tablespoon of orange zest
1 tablespoon pure vanilla extract

Preparation time: 25 minutes plus 35-40 minutes chilling
Bake time: approximate: 12-15 minutes Makes 1 Roulade

Method:
• In a large mixing bowl, beat the egg yolks and sugar until thick and light pale in color. In another bowl add the cake flour, and sift the cocoa powder into the cake flour.

• Add a little of the combined flour and cocoa powder to the egg yolk batter and combine well.

• Use a mixing bowl with the whisk attachment, whisk the egg whites until foamy, then add ¼ cup of sugar slowly and whisk until it holds stiff peaks.

• Fold half of the egg whites carefully into your egg yolk batter mixture, add the remainder of the combined cocoa and flour mixture and fold in the rest of your egg whites carefully until all is combined.

• Pour the batter into a prepared baking tray lined with baking paper, spread batter evenly and smoothly with a spatula, bake in a 350°F oven for about 12-15 minutes. Then remove from the oven and let stand for about 5 minutes. After this, invert the cake onto a sheet of wax paper or baking paper sprinkled with a little sugar (this will prevent it from sticking to the paper).

• Roll up the wax paper together with the cake until you mak a log, set aside, and fully cool.

• Using a mixing bowl or hand mixer, add heavy cream, orange zest, and vanilla, whisk until creamy, then add the sifted confectioners' sugar and continue to whisk until creamy and fluffy. Refrigerate until you are ready to spread onto your cake.

• Gently unroll the cake, spread the orange cream evenly - b careful not to overfill - smooth it out, then roll up from the shorter side of the roulade, keeping the cake together with the wax paper until you form it into a log. Make sure to tighten the sides of the wax paper while rolling the log.

• Refrigerate for about 45-50 minutes or longer. When you a ready to serve, remove the wax paper, put your roulade on a plate or platter, dust with confectioners sugar, then slice into circles with a sharp knife. Serve with fresh berries if desired.

Pavlova with Cream and Mixed Berries

4 room temperature egg whites
1 1/2 cups very fine white sugar or castor sugar
2 tsp lemon juice or vinegar
1/2 tsp vanilla or almond extract
2 tsp corn starch
1 cup heavy cream
1/2 cup confectioner's sugar
1 tbsp mascarpone cheese
A few strawberries, blackberries, blueberries, raspberries
A few mint leaves (for decorating)

Bake at 266°F for 10 minutes then turn the temperature down to 100°F for 90 minutes. (1 1/2 hours)

- Separate the egg whites from the yolk. Add your egg whites to a stand mixer with the whisk attachment. Start on low speed until bubbles have formed, then on high speed to incorporate more air to form soft foamy peaks.

- Add your castor sugar a spoonful at a time on medium speed till all is added, making sure not to deflate the egg whites. Turn the mixer to a high speed until stiff peaks are formed and it holds its shape.

- Add the lemon juice and vanilla or almond extract and mix to combine. Add your cornstarch and fold with a metal spoon.

- Line a tray with parchment paper, pour the meringue into the middle of the tray and use a palette knife to shape into a circle, then scoop out the centre, spread the sides out nicely and smooth out. To form a beautiful pattern, drag your palette knife up the sides at an angle to the top.

- Scoop the centre out, leaving space for cream filling and mixed berries. Put the pavlova into the oven and follow the baking instructions.

- After your Pavlova has completely cooled down, take it out of the oven onto a platter and set it aside.

IMPORTANT: To ensure a beautiful pavlova, after turning the oven off, let it cool down completely. Failure to let it completely cool will result in the meringue cracking, so leave it in the oven to cool completely before removing the meringue.

Whipped Cream Filling:

Combine 1 cup of heavy cream, ½ cup of confectioner's sugar and 1 tbsp of mascarpone cheese using a stand mixer. Whip until creamy and light. Fill the middle of your pavlova with your cream, arranging some of your mixed berries, then add second layer of cream and arrange more mixed berries until looks high and beautiful and full of mixed berries. Add your mint leaves for a pretty decoration, serve and enjoy!

Red Wine Poached Pears with Cognac Cream

4 medium firm Bosc or Bartlett pears
3 cups of red wine (suggesting Zinfandel)
1 1⁄2 cup of sugar
2 tbsp honey
Juice and zest of 1 lemon
1 tsp orange zest
1 cinnamon stick
1 star anise
4 cloves

Whipped Cognac Cream:
1⁄2 cup cold heavy whipping cream
1 tsp pure vanilla extract
1 tsp cognac
4 tbsp powdered sugar

- Peel the pears leaving them whole with the stems on. Set aside in a bowl with the lemon juice.

- In a large saucepan, add wine, cinnamon stick, star anise, cloves, citrus zest, sugar, honey, and bring to a boil.

- Add the pears, reduce the heat to a simmer, and using a large spoon, keep tossing the wine mixture over the pears ever so often and poach for about 35-40 minutes until they change color. Use a skewer to test for softness.

- Remove the pears with a slotted spoon. Continue to simmer the liquid to reduce it, then cool.
  Pour liquid over the pears and refrigerate overnight, or up to 2 days.

- Before serving, remove from refrigerator, thaw to room temperature, and serve with whipped cognac cream and mint leaves for decoration.

Whipped Cognac Cream:
- Using a hand mixer, whip heavy cream with powdered sugar, vanilla extract and cognac until it forms soft peaks.

- Serve to your guests. It makes a beautiful and elegant dessert.

Madeleines

Preparation time: 20-25 minutes
Baking time: 10-12 minutes
Serves 12

¾ cup of sifted flour
¼ tsp baking powder
2 eggs at room temperature
½ cups granulated sugar
7 tbsp of butter, melted
1 teaspoon finely grated orange zest
1 teaspoon vanilla extract
2 tablespoons confectioners' sugar for dusting

Method

• Using a mixer or hand mixer, add eggs, sugar, vanilla, orange zest; whisk until thick and pale in color.

• Fold in the flour into the egg mixture then add the melted butter into the mixture and fold well to incorporate.

• Cover with plastic wrap and refrigerate for about 20-30 minutes.

• Preheat oven to 350°F and lightly grease and flour Madeleine tins.

• Remove the batter from the refrigerator, add about 1 tbsp of batter into the madeleine molds. Be careful not to overfill.

• Bake for 10-12 minutes or until slightly golden around edges.

• Carefully remove from tins and place on a wire rack for cooling.

• When completely cooled, dust with confectioners' sugar and serve.

These cookies are best served same day but can be kept in an airtight container up to two days.

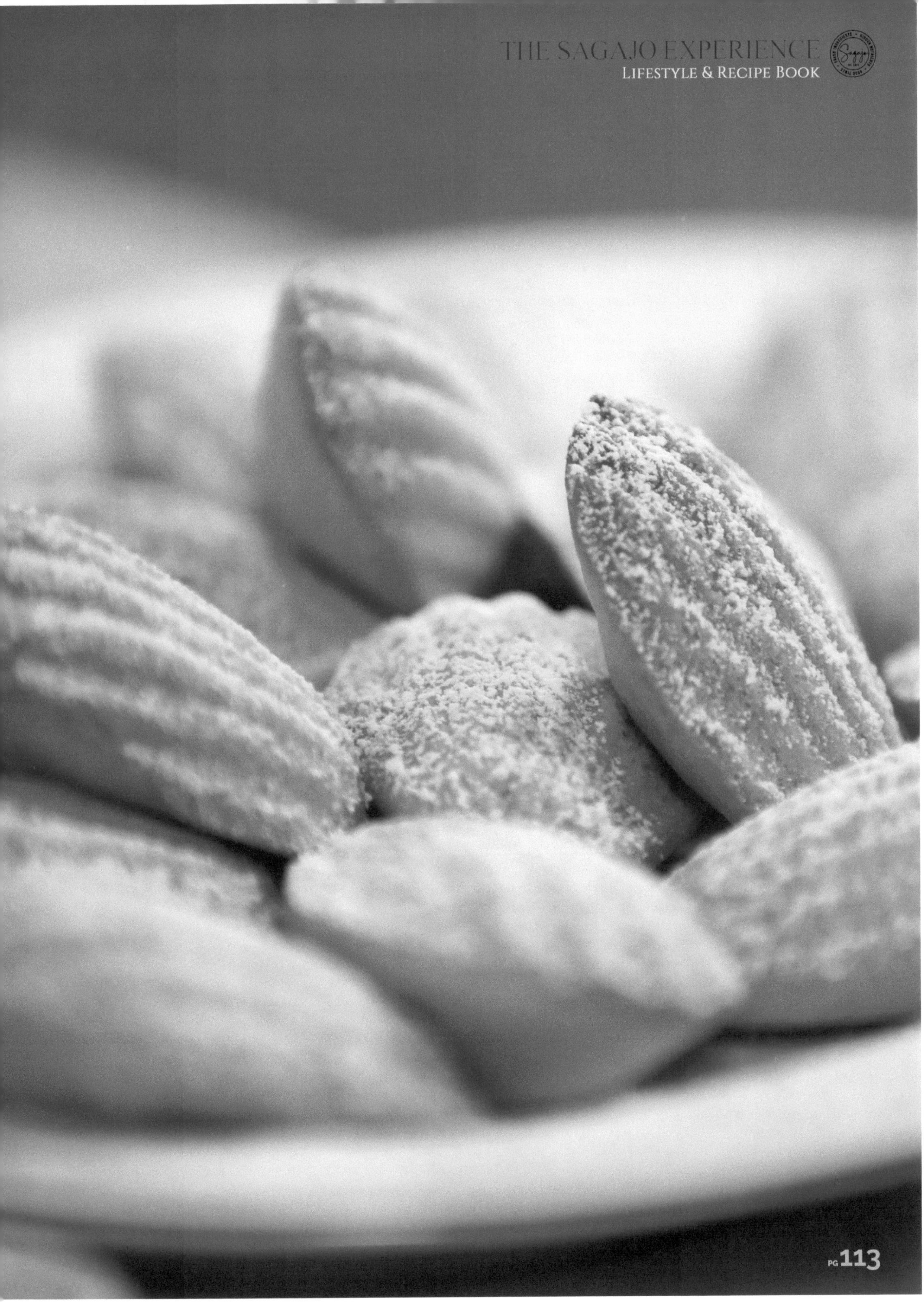

ood and Wine Pairings

me, living is cause for celebration, and life presents many uses for celebrations, whether they be holidays, anniversa-s or any other special occasion. For every one of these, you ould consider the way that delicious food will be paired with ulent wines. When I consider what to put on the menu, I ways try to do a few well balanced, delicious and appealing shes rather than many. This allows me to have wines that pair ith everything from my appetizer to the dessert. Organizing d planning ahead is definitely a must! I like giving a selection wines that vary from subtle roses, to crisp refreshing whites d bold reds. When you pair food with wine that suits your late, it feels as though the meal was catered to you, and at's exactly how I want my guests to feel!

hroughout my book I have created recipes for you to which u can easily apply your own style and create unique dining xperiences. The same applies to making wine choices.

ke my herb roasted rack of lamb with lavender for example, hich has a more delicate flavor than beef. I'd pair the lamb ith a medium bodied wine such as a Malbec, Syrah or Shiraz at will add a well rounded intensity of flavor to compliment e lamb.

hen I prepare my flavorful honey glazed Cornish hens, the icy white meat would pair perfectly with white wines like a auvignon Blanc or a Chardonnay. There are times I also like to erve the hens with Pinot noir when I think it would add lance to the overall meal, if I'm serving heavier sides.

not noir is also a classic pairing with a succulent roasted duck. balances out the fattiness of the duck with its fruity notes and avor! If you can't already tell, Pinot noir is one of the many ines I tend to regularly have in my wine cooler because it's so ersatile and can please any palate.

Let's talk about another one of my favorites- the seafood pasta. This is another recipe that you will be able to easily recreate for your entertainment pleasure. This dish is best paired with Pinot Grigio or even something a little bubbly like Proscecco. These wines have a refreshing and slightly bitter note that's needed to bring balance when working with sweet and salty sea foods.

If you're a seafood lover like me or you're a pescatarian, my seared Sea-bass will definitely entice your taste buds! Because seafood is so delicate, I offer the pairings of Pinot Grigio, Char-donnay, Champagne or sparkling wines - something refreshing that adds a bit of zestiness and lends a perfect balance that will awaken the briny flavors of the seafood, vegetables and sauces.

I know it may seem daunting, but learning to pair wines with foods is a skill you'll always use in the kitchen. You'll enjoy your meals to the fullest, your guests will be impressed and your time in the kitchen will be even that more enjoyable. My advice is to start thinking of wines as you arrange your menu. Create a small-scale test menu so you can experimentally pair different foods and wine flavors.

These are some of my on-hand pantry favorites. It helps for quick preparations whether it's just baking, easy lunches or dinners, or spur-of-the-moment entertaining.

Produce

- Sweet whole onions
- Purple onions
- Lemons, limes, oranges, grapefruits
- Fresh garlic
- Bay Leaves
- Thyme Bunches (container ones are great)

Dry Goods

- Assorted varieties of dry pasta like Fettuccini, Bow Tie, Orecchtti, Spaghetti, Ziti
- Unbleached All Purpose Flour
- Self-rising flour
- Corn Meal Flour
- Almond Flour
- Arborio Rice
- Basmati Rice
- Panko plain bread crumbs
- Active dry yeast
- Instant yeast
- Baking Powder
- Baking Soda
- Cocoa Powder
- Pure Vanilla Extract
- Corn Starch Powder
- Semi-sweet chocolate chips
- White Sugar
- Dark Brown Sugar
- Light Brown Sugar
- Whole Pecans
- Walnuts

Spices

Cardamom Pods
Cloves
Cinnamon Sticks
Vanilla Bean Pods
Star Anise
Fresh whole Nutmeg

Red Pepper Flakes
Saffron Threads
Saffron Powder
Curry Powder
Cumin
Whole Tri Color Peppercorns and Black Peppercorns (I like the flavor blend of the tri-color peppercorns)
Sea Salt
Kosher Salt
Garlic Salt
Garlic Powder

Refrigerated

Salted and unsalted butter
Organic whole milk
Half and half milk
Heavy whipping cream
Buttermilk
Sour cream
Cream cheese
Cheddar Cheese
Whole romaine lettuces
Whole radishes
Olives

Oils

Extra virgin olive oil
Sunflower Oil
Vegetable oil
Canola oil
Avocado oil

I try to keep my oil supplies well stocked...

Vinegar

White Vinegar
Apple Cider Vinegar
Balsamic Vinegar

OVEN TEMPERATURE CONVERSIONS

CHEF SAGAJO

GAS MARK	DEGREE CELCIUS °C	DEGREE CELSIUS FAN °C	DEGREE FAHRENHEIT °F
1/4	110°C	100°C	225 °F
1/2	120°C	110°C	250 °F
1	140°C	120°C	275 °F
2	150°C	130°C	300 °F
3	170°C	140°C	325 °F
4	180°C	160°C	350 °F
5	190 °C	170°C	375 °F
6	200 °C	180°C	400 °F
7	220 °C	200°C	425 °F
8	230 °C	210°C	450 °F
9	240 °C	220°C	475 °F
10	260 °C	240°C	500 °F

INDEX

ACKNOWLEDGEMENTS

To my luv luv Gordon A Berment

Throughout the years you have been my rock of support. Your love and commitment to me and our beautiful children is like no other, my luv. You have stood by me through all my endeavours and supported my vision. I enjoy spending time in the kitchen with you, as my sous chef, and no one can ask for a better sous chef. You are my taste tester and let's not forget, my biggest supporting fan. I could not have done any of this without you, my luv.

So, thank you for loving and supporting me.

To my wonderful children Sasha Lillion, Gabrielle Berment and Jonathan Berment.

Without you there would be no SAGAJO! You are the bright stars thats help my light to shine. Cooking meals for you and spending time with you all, in our kitchen is priceless. When I decided to write the Sagajo experiences you were all very supportive and caring. Sasha, my oldest, who helped with some of my writing, there are no words to express my love and gratitude. I enjoy our special moments together in the kitchen with our beautiful Isla. My Gabby, you are one of the biggest taste testers and recipe creators who enjoys making my recipes ......dear I say; you LOVE when I make pastries. Jono, my sweet son, loves to add a pinch of this and a pinch of that. You always enjoy when I prepare slow cooked meals and grilled steaks–You are definitely the meat lover in our family.

To my beautiful grandchildren Isla Lillion, Maverick Lillion and Mason Kratka.

Words cannot express all the love and joy you have brought to our lives– I love creating our dinners, especially when we gather for dinners and the holidays to celebrate the pure joy of love, family, food and fun. Each of you are like ingredients that brings the perfect flavors to my life.

To my Sons-in-Law Calvin Lillion and Charles Kratka.

Thanks for always being there with ideas supporting and believing in me during one of my biggest projects. You guys definitely cheered me to the finish line.

Thankful to Krystal Chung

who supported me from the very beginning through this whole project. You believed in my goal and vision and was always willing to assist, thank you for all that you did. You are so special to our family.

To My Dear Friends Sheri Weinman, Sheryl Grant, Sheri Mantzoor, Melissa Kratka.

I cannot thank you enough for being there for me and supporting my bookproject. You gave of your time and I appreciate it. Your friendship means so much to me ladies, a huge thank you.

To Michelle Borel Media Ltd and Virago Global Publishing LLC team.

Without your incredible support in getting this project started and helping to bring my dreams and vision of the Sagajo experience to life. This entire process was a huge one, especially for me, but your focus and dedication was truly awesome. I am happy that you always understood my clear vision. The Photography, Editing and Illustration team was incredible and my food looked awesome!! Each page looks beautiful and I cannot thank you all enough.

To Meryl Moss Media Group and Book Trib.

Thank you for getting my book to the right audiences, guiding and supporting my vision for my book with the publicity and marketing campaign. The collaboration to help me to expose the Sagajo experiences to others. I could not have done this without you and your awesome team. Thank you.

My gratitude and heartfelt thanks to all my family and friends who stood by me through the end. To those who choose to have this book, I hope that the recipes will inspire you to gather and entertain with joy.

Thank you all! *Chef Sagajo Debbie Wilson-Berment*

Printed in the USA
CPSIA information can be obtained
at www.ICGtesting.com
LVHW062351030324
773189LV00006B/49